PIANO · VOCAL · GUITAR

STEVEN CURTIS CHAPMAN: SPEECHLESS

ISBN 0-634-00971-0

HAL·LEONARD®
CORPORATION
7777 W. BLUEMOUND RD. P.O. BOX 13819 MILWAUKEE, WI 53213

Visit Hal Leonard Online at
www.halleonard.com

STEVEN CURTIS CHAPMAN: SPEECHLESS

DIVE

Words and Music by
STEVEN CURTIS CHAPMAN

The long a-wait-ed rains have fall-en hard up-on the thirst-y ground;
There is a su-per-nat-ral pow-er in this might-y riv-er's flow.

Come on, ___ let's go. ___ I'm div - ing in; I'm go - ing deep,

SPEECHLESS

Words and Music by STEVEN CURTIS CHAPMAN
and GEOFF MOORE

24

THE CHANGE

Words and Music by STEVEN CURTIS CHAPMAN
and JAMES ISAAC ELLIOTT

Well, I got my-self _ a tee - shirt that

34

GREAT EXPECTATIONS

Words and Music by
STEVEN CURTIS CHAPMAN

The morn-ing finds __ me here __ at heav - en's door, __

a place I've been so man - y times __ be - fore.

Original key: Ab minor. This edition has been transposed up one half-step to be more playable.

We've been in - vit -

NEXT 5 MINUTES

Words and Music by STEVEN CURTIS CHAPMAN
and ADAM ANDERS

Moderately fast

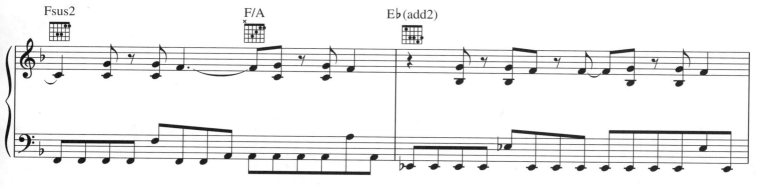

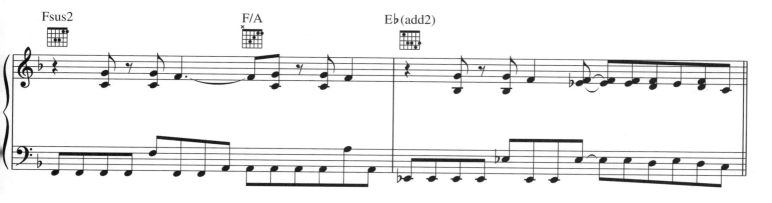

FINGERPRINTS OF GOD

Words and Music by
STEVEN CURTIS CHAPMAN

D A/C# Bm A Gmaj9
can see the fin - ger - prints of God, and
G A Em9 A7 F#7/A#
4 fr
I know it's true. You're a mas - ter-piece that all cre - a - tion
Bm D/A E/G# Bm7 E7 Em7
2 fr
qui - et - ly ap - plauds and you're cov - ered with the fin -
Gm6 D A/C# Bm9 Bm/A
3 fr
- ger - prints of God. You are cov -

THE INVITATION

Words and Music by STEVEN CURTIS CHAPMAN
and GEOFF MOORE

In the pal - ace in the land _____ of mer - cy the
So I stood out - side the gates _____ and trem - bled in my

King looked _ out _____ from His throne. ___
rags of _____ un - worth - i - ness, ___

So now _____ will you come with _ me ____

to where the gates ___ swing _ o - pen wide?

WHATEVER

Words and Music by
STEVEN CURTIS CHAPMAN

I made a   list,
I formed a   plan;
So strike a   match,

wrote down from A   to __ Z   all the ways   I __ thought __ that You could best   use   me;
it seemed to make   good __ sense   I laid it out   for __ You, __ so sure You'd be   con - vinced.
set fire __ to   the __ list   of all my good   in - ten - tions, all my pre-con - ceived __ i -

I DO BELIEVE

Words and Music by
STEVEN CURTIS CHAPMAN

Sit - ting in a traf - fic jam,
As these can be con-fus - ing times,

84

WHAT I REALLY WANT TO SAY

Words and Music by
STEVEN CURTIS CHAPMAN

WITH HOPE

Words and Music by
STEVEN CURTIS CHAPMAN

96

We let _____ go _____ with hope. _____ *Whispered: Yes, we believe.*

THE JOURNEY

Words and Music by STEVEN CURTIS CHAPMAN
and J.A.C. REDFORD

Moderately fast

BE STILL AND KNOW

Words and Music by
STEVEN CURTIS CHAPMAN

CONTEMPORARY CHRISTIAN FOLIOS
available from Hal Leonard

SUSAN ASHTON – SO FAR ... THE BEST OF SUSAN ASHTON
12 songs, featuring her #1 hits. Songs include: Stand • Hide Or Seek • Here In My Heart • Grand Canyon • and more.

00306061 Piano / Vocal / Guitar $12.95

SUSAN ASHTON
Matching folio featuring: Agree To Disagree • Hold The Intangible • Remember Not • A Rose Is A Rose • Waiting For Your Love To Come Down • and more. Arranged for keyboard and medium voice with chord symbols.

00306099 Piano / Vocal / Guitar................................$10.95

MICHAEL CARD – JOY IN THE JOURNEY
Matching folio to his compilation of 10 years of hits. 18 songs, including: El Shaddai • The Final Word • Known By Scars • and more.

00306152 Piano / Vocal / Guitar $12.95

STEVEN CURTIS CHAPMAN – HEAVEN IN THE REAL WORLD
Matching folio with 12 songs, including: Heaven In The Real World • King Of The Jungle • The Mountain • Love And Learn • and more.

00306151 Piano / Vocal / Guitar $14.95

STEVEN CURTIS CHAPMAN – THE MUSIC OF CHRISTMAS
12 traditional favorites, including: Angels We Have Heard On High • Carol Of The Bells • Interlude: The Music Of Christmas • Our God Is With Us • Precious Promise • This Baby • and more.

00313031 Piano / Vocal / Guitar $14.95

STEVEN CURTIS CHAPMAN – SIGNS OF LIFE
Matching folio to the newest release from this best-selling, award-winning artist. 12 songs, including: Celebrate You • Free • Lord Of The Dance • What Would I Say • Signs Of Life • and more.

00306119 Piano / Vocal / Guitar $14.95

STEVEN CURTIS CHAPMAN – TWENTY FAVORITES
This folio, complete with photos, features 20 songs from his entire career, including: Don't Let The Fire Die • For The Sake Of The Call • Go There With You • The Great Adventure • I Will Be Here • More To This Life • My Turn Now • When You Are A Soldier • and more.
00306150 Piano / Vocal / Guitar $14.95

DELIRIOUS – SONGS FROM CUTTING EDGE
15 songs, including: All I Want Is You • Did You Feel the Mountain Tremble? • I Could Sing of Your Love Forever • I'm Not Ashamed • I've Found Jesus • Lord, You Have My Heart • and more.

00306243 Piano / Vocal / Guitar $17.95

STEVE GREEN – THE FIRST NOEL
Matching folio to Steve Green's newest Christmas recording. Songs include: Midnight Clear • Jesu, Light Of Lights • What Child Is This? • Rose Of Bethlehem • and six others.

00306115 Piano / Vocal / Guitar $14.95

ANDY GRIFFITH – I LOVE TO TELL THE STORY
Souvenir matching folio to the popular recording. Contains photos and background information on Andy plus notes on the hymns. 23 songs, including: How Great Thou Art • The Old Rugged Cross • Sweet Hour Of Prayer • Wayfaring Stranger • What A Friend We Have In Jesus • and more.
00306116 Piano / Vocal / Guitar $14.95

CHERI KEAGGY – MY FAITH WILL STAY
Matching folio with 10 songs, including: Beautiful Little Girl • He Will Look After You • Heavenly Father • In Remembrance Of Me • Keep On Shinin' • Lay It Down • The Love Of God • My Faith Will Stay • Sweet Peace Of God • We All Need Jesus.

00306107 Piano / Vocal / Guitar $16.95

GIVING YOU THE REST OF MY LIFE
13 contemporary Christian classics from Steven Curtis Chapman, Susan Ashton, Steve Green, Michael English, and more. Songs include: All I Ever Wanted • Friends For Life • Go There With You • Over And Over • Wedding Song (There Is Love) • and more.

00313068 Piano / Vocal / Guitar $10.95